The Little Book of

Love & Light

Lots of love & light
to you always!
Matahi ♡

The Little Book of

Love
&
Light

Natalia Colman

Published in 2017 by Style Specialists
West Yorkshire, United Kingdom

Text © Natalia Colman 2017
Illustrations: Natalia Colman
Cover design and interior design: Keith Loveday

The moral rights of the author have been asserted. All rights reserved. No part of this book may be reproduced by any mechanical, photographic or electronic process, or in any form of a photographic recording; nor may it be stored in a retrieval system, transmitted or otherwise copied for public or private use, other than for 'fair use' as brief quotations embodied in articles, reviews, without prior written permission of the publisher.

Every reasonable attempt has been made to identify owners of copyright.
Errors or omissions will be corrected in subsequent editions.

The information given within this book should not be treated as a substitute for professional medical advice; always consult a medical practitioner. Any use of information in this book is at the reader's discretion and risk. Neither the author nor the publisher can be held responsible for any loss, claim or damage arising from the use, or misuse, or the suggestions made, or the failure to take medical advice.

A catalogue record for this book is available from the British Library.
ISBN 978-0-9570968-6-8

Printed and bound by The Marstan Press Limited, Princes Street, Bexleyheath, Kent, DA7 4BJ.

To Estella,
the loveliest and brightest of stars

Contents

Page Number

	Introduction	9
1.	You, glorious you	15
2.	Remember where you came from	29
3.	Patience dear one…patience	41
4.	Love, love, love	57
5.	Be authentic	71
6.	You are very wise indeed	81
7.	Keeping the light on	93
	Further reading	111

Introduction

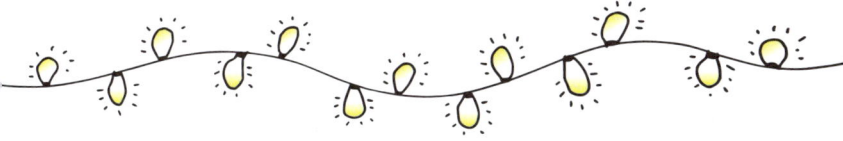

Love and light! You've probably heard this expression a lot. We often say it without really thinking what it means. I chose it for the title of this book, because the words and the essence of love and light capture everything life is about.

Love makes the world go around because love is in everything we do, from the people in our lives, to the food that we eat; the clothes we wear, the places that are closest to our hearts and the music we listen to. Yet, love is about so much more than that. Love is the most powerful emotion of all. It gives us a reason to keep going. It heals and it empowers us to make the most of every day on the planet. Light is all about courage; having the courage to shine as brightly as you can, even when everything around you feels dark, you're comparing yourself to others and you don't feel particularly shiny at all. It's about knowing you're powerful, remembering this fact and claiming that power every day. Having the courage to reclaim your power when others try to take it away from you or when you disempower yourself. When you have love and light in your life, when you love and approve of yourself, when you're doing what you love every day, when you're shining your light as brightly as you possibly can, that's when you're getting the very best out of your own life. Imagine this: if everyone else was doing the same, how much more amazing would the world be?

I will be honest and say that my life wasn't always so light filled. For many years, I definitely didn't love myself or feel loved by other people. I felt lonely and isolated and thought everything that was 'happening to me' was some kind of punishment for not being good enough. It was only when I stopped searching outside of myself to make my life better, that I discovered true happiness and inner peace was there all along.

I discovered a secret that I want to share with you: **to live a life filled with love and light, then you have to notice the magic going on around you right now.** When you spot it, give thanks for it every day, because magic is everywhere. It's hiding in the delicious froth on top of your cappuccino. It's in the cute little whiskers on next door's cat. It's hiding under the comfy covers on your bed, the safe haven that helps you relax and forget about the troubles of the day. Magic is all around you. Recognise it and give thanks to it. Everyone likes to be appreciated, especially magic!

You see, when you find perfection within the imperfect and release expectations and control of outcomes, magic happens there too. You'll find you accept and love yourself far more. When you focus on your personal happiness and become more open and honest about who you are and what you want to do with your life, you'll find the joy you've been looking for all along. That's how I found my joy, or perhaps it found me, simply because I was ready to accept it.

It feels like you're ready to accept the love and light you deserve too. I guess that's why you're reading this book right now. I want this little book to be a gift to inspire you every day. Read it from cover to cover or just open it randomly, look at the words on that page, let them to guide you and make you think. Turn to this book if you're feeling lower than a snake's belly or you just don't know what to do next. Read it when you're happy and want to lift yourself up even further. Share the quotes, messages and stories in this book with your friends. It might just be the shot in the arm they need to brighten their day. Most of all, keep this book close by and look at it regularly. You'll notice different messages on different days, because life is a series of ups and downs and we all need encouragement along the journey.

If any of the words in this book resonate with you, help to lift your spirits and keep you marching bravely forward, then my mission has been accomplished.

Love and light to you,

Chapter One

You, glorious you

"Maybe my best isn't as good as someone else's, but for a lot of people, my best is enough.
Most importantly, for me it's enough."

– Lindsey Stirling

You are amazing. Did you know that?

Maybe you remember this from time to time. Then you do something you're not that proud of and you beat yourself up about it, or someone else tells you you're not good enough…then what? You most probably start telling yourself you're anything but amazing.

Now, here's the thing I'd like you to remember: there's no one quite like you. You're a complete individual, just as no two fingerprints are ever exactly alike in every detail. Your upbringing, the way you look, your skills and talents and your life path are all completely unique. That's why it's impossible to compare yourself to someone else. No yardstick exists to take a fair and accurate measurement.

What if you started to concentrate on where YOU want to go instead of looking around you at where other people are headed?

What if your definition of success was the best one and the only one?

How much more accomplished would you feel?

When you take the pressure off yourself to compete with other people, that's when you can begin to concentrate on what's important to you; to up your game and achieve the results you want on your own terms. You'll also find that a funny thing starts happening: you begin to love and approve of yourself a whole lot more. Life immediately begins to feel so much more enjoyable when you go from beating yourself up, to becoming your own best friend.

Give yourself permission to be amazing.
Try it. Today. Get out of your own way.
What are you waiting for?

> "I'm okay just the way I am. I play my position in the world. I catch the ball when it is thrown my way. I don't always have to make the crowd go wild or get a standing ovation. It's good enough to just catch the ball or even to do my best to catch it. Good enough means that I finally enjoy playing the game."

– Jenni Schaefer

> *"That is part of the beauty of all literature. You discover that your longings are universal longings, that you're not lonely and isolated from anyone. You belong."*

– F. Scott Fitzgerald

Begin by building your tribe

Tribe / noun: a class or set of persons, especially one with strong common traits or interests.

We all need a tribe. I love this word and I love being part of one.

Since time began, people came together in tribes and had a common identity and a strong culture; a collective way of doing things. Each member had different strengths and roles that made the tribe more powerful. Although we're not officially organised into tribes these days, I believe that modern-day power lies in connecting with like-minded people who just 'get' who you are and what you do. There are over seven billion human beings in the world, so there are plenty of your fellow tribespeople to choose from. Go seek them out, bond with them and hold them close.

No matter how old you are, don't try to fit in where you don't belong. Why twist yourself out of shape to attempt to be someone you're not? You are perfect just as you are. Discover that perfection within yourself and hang out with those people who see it in you too.

In days gone by, tribespeople lived alongside one another, but with the wonders of the internet and a healthy dose of positive thinking and imagination, you can have your tribe around you always. You don't need money, miracles or a time machine.

How do you go about building your tribe? Look around for the people who think on the same wavelength as you.

Seek out the ones who are doing what you want to do and doing it in the very best way.

Appreciate their talents, see how they can lift you up and inspire you to be better, so you can be an inspiration to other people. As Silicon Valley, Venture Capitalist Scott Weiss says *"...track down the best people in the world...and surround yourself with them."*

You might be thinking, *"Okay, there are people who I'd like to be around and align myself with, but what if they don't feel the same way or they are completely inaccessible?"* The other important thing to note about assembling your tribe is they don't have to be close by or even known to you.

Imagine for a moment: who are the people living or dead that you most look up to. Whose life, personality and achievements do you appreciate?

Two of my tribe members are Oprah and the architect Frank Lloyd Wright. I don't know Oprah personally (yet) and Frank Lloyd Wright passed away before I was even born. That doesn't stop me from loving their work, their philosophy on life and their sense of humour. I can relate to their struggles and I just know if we were stuck on a desert island together, we'd get on like a house on fire – that would be my idea of heaven.

Oprah grew up in poverty, experienced horrific emotional turmoil, yet managed to overcome it to become one of the most famous people in the world. She uses her wealth and status to do good, giving away several hundred million dollars to charities and education. Most of all, despite her immense success and power, she is down-to-earth, humorous, inquisitive and shares great warmth and empathy with whomever she interviews.

Why do I love Frank Lloyd Wright so much? Well it's because he was considered to be the greatest American architect of all time, yet the first 40 years of his life were beset with divorce, tragedy and scandal. He lived to the ripe old age of 91 and didn't achieve his most notable success until he was in his 60s. His drive, tenacity, creativity and downright quirkiness fascinates me and the legacy he created in the fourth act of his life, inspires me never to give up.

Your own idols have so much to contribute to your development. Just look at how they approach life, how they've overcome obstacles, how they project themselves, the things they've achieved and the way they did it. Let those things inform you as you go through life. Ask yourself: *"What would (insert the name of your guru) do about this problem?"*

"What advice would they give me today?"

I can guarantee that gathering your tribe will help you make more sense of your world, especially on those days when nothing makes much sense at all.

> "Don't waste your time being what someone wants you to become...find your tribe. They will allow you to be you, while you dance in the rain."

– Shannon L. Adler

Stay grounded

> **"Flying starts from the ground.
> The more grounded you are,
> the higher you fly."**

– J.R. Rim

It's all-too easy to buckle under the stress of what we consider to be failure, or when life isn't treating us kindly. That's why it's so important to stay grounded and put our roots down as deeply as we can.

In the 1980s there was an experiment called the biodome. A perfect living environment for human beings, plant, and animal life was created in the Arizona desert. This consisted of a huge glass dome, an artificially-controlled environment, with purified air and water and filtered light. The scientists who created it thought that it would offer the perfect conditions for trees, fruits and vegetables to grow. Everything seemed to go according to plan except for one thing: when the trees that were planted grew to be a certain height, they would topple over. The scientists couldn't understand why this was happening. Until one day, they suddenly realised that one important natural element was missing: and that was wind. The scientists discovered that when wind blows against trees, this causes their root systems to grow deeper into the soil, which then supports the tree as it grows taller.

What can we learn from the biodome experiment? If you're honest, don't you secretly wish that everyday life was like being on the inside of the biodome? No unexpected storms to test you or no outside influences challenging you? I don't know anyone who enjoys having to stand strong against the elements that push against us, and equally those very stressors are the things that have made you who you are. They built your character and gave you wisdom. Without them, you would crash and fall just like those biodome trees.

One of the biggest problems with making mistakes and experiencing the heavy weather life throws at us is that we tend to dwell on it. We carry it around like a badge of honour, lest we forget. Instead of drawing all the wisdom and goodness from it, we use those mistakes or painful times to taunt ourselves with shame and worry.

My daughter came home from a motivational talk at her college by Sports Psychologist, David Sammel. She told me about a great analogy he'd used. I loved it so much I had to share it in this book. He said that all the mistakes and problems we encounter in life are like oranges. The lesson within those mistakes and problems is like taking the juice out of the orange. It nourishes us and we get something valuable from every last drop, no matter how sweet or bitter it might taste. When we've squeezed all the juice from that orange what do we do? Sometimes we throw it away, but way too often we put the dead orange skin into our rucksack and carry it around with us. One or two oranges won't make a difference but year upon year, the weight of all of these orange skins becomes a very heavy burden indeed.

Making a mistake, enduring a problem, going through emotional pain, doesn't make you wrong and you don't have to make yourself suffer forever more. Find a rubbish bin, waste disposal or compost heap and cast away those dead orange carcases. Take only the juice from the oranges that life serves you and see their blessing. Then give thanks for all the turbulent weather in your life. It's given you the depth you need to keep growing and stay standing taller than ever.

> ### "The finest steel has to go through the hottest fire."

– Richard M. Nixon

Notes to self...

Chapter Two

Remember where you came from

> "The biggest challenge after success is shutting up about it."

– Criss Jami

Success can be just as much of a challenge to your character as failure.

It's way too easy to get carried away with your own self-importance when you achieve success. Never forget where you came from, no matter how high up the worldly ladder you climb. We all must start somewhere, even the people who we perceive as being wildly successful had their dragons to slay and hurdles to overcome.

It's not important how much money or status you have, the true measure of your success is how kind you are.

Never look down on other people. You don't know what it's like to walk in their shoes. We are all going through our own struggles and everyone has their back story, if you just take the time to see beyond the veneer.

I want to share the story of Chinese man, He Rongfeng. It's a heart-warming tale of exactly the type of human kindness this world needs.

At 17 years old, Rongfeng had ventured to the city to find work. He needed to earn money to send back home to support his family. The plan backfired as no one would employ him and the little money he had soon ran out.

He ended up homeless and sleeping rough on the streets of Taizhou in China. He searched endlessly for work but became dirtier and more unkempt, lessening his chances of success with every day that passed.

By the time a kind-hearted noodle shop owner called Dai Xingfen came across him, he was emotionally and physically broken. She took him in and gave him food and a place to stay for the night. In the morning, she called a friend in another town who could set Rongfeng up with a job and gave him the money for his train fare to get out of the city. Before sending him on his way she told him: *"It's okay not to have a lot of money, but always strive to be a good person"*.

Rongfeng did just that. This lady's message and her act of kindness inspired him to make a better life for himself. He took advantage of the small window of opportunity he'd been given, worked hard from that day and went on to become a wealthy business tycoon. Rongfeng always credited this lady with helping him to turn his life around. This was something he never forgot and he spent years searching for the woman who had helped him.

Some twenty years later, Rongfeng was finally able to track her down. He attempted to give her £100,000 because he was adamant that if it hadn't been for Dai's kindness, he wouldn't be where he was today.

So modest was Dai, she turned down the money, but Rongfeng would not be put off, he returned after having a special plaque made for her. The saying on the plaque was this: **'Gratitude. As heavy as a mountain'**.

> "If the only prayer you ever say
> in your entire life is thank you,
> it will be enough."

– Meister Eckhart

Change & grow

> **When the winds of change blow, some people build walls and others build windmills**

– Chinese Proverb

Change isn't always welcome. Ask a caterpillar about that. I'm sure it appreciates becoming a butterfly in the end, but the process it goes through sure looks painful to me.

Why do we often resist and fear change in our lives? Our resistance to change is strongly connected to what scientists call the lizard brain. This is the oldest part of the **brain**, the **brain** stem, where our survival instincts such as aggression and fear ("flight or fight") sit. It's the primitive part of human beings. The part that drives you to eat and be safe. The resistance is the voice in the back of your head telling you to give up, be careful, go slow, compromise, stay at home. If you allow it, the lizard of fear will move into your head and take up precious imagination space.

Do you really want the lizard to be in control of your life? It's okay when you have a busy road to cross or when you're weighing up the pros and cons of eating the piece of chicken that's two days past the eat-by date. I applaud the lizard brain on those occasions, but when it is stifling you from going on an adventure, from meeting new people, or making you so afraid you won't act on your dreams, that's when you need to tell your lizard brain to take a hike.

I remember a time when I was asked to teach jewellery making on a cruise ship. I wasn't so sure about it until I found out that the ship would be going on a seven-day cruise through the Norwegian Fjords, a place I'd always wanted to visit. I would also be able to take someone with me on the trip. When I discovered that, I jumped at the chance. Unfortunately, the week before the cruise, I broke up with my boyfriend who was due to accompany me. I asked all my friends if they'd like to take his place. Everyone was either terrified of the sea or couldn't get time off at short notice.

I tried to cancel the trip, but the cruise company informed me it was too late to back out now because I'd already signed the teaching contract. I shuddered as I realised there was nothing for it; I would have to go on my own.

On the day of the cruise it took me five hours to drive to the port. With every minute of the journey that passed I was feeling more and more anxious. When I saw the massive ship on the quayside my stomach flipped over and I started to shake and hyperventilate. My lizard brain had me well and truly in its grip. I still don't know to this day how I managed to prise myself out of the car and climb aboard that ship, but somehow, I did.

Then something amazing happened. It was as though the Universe decided to reward me for my bravery (or for overcoming my cowardice). Those seven days turned out to be one of the best weeks of my life. I made lots of new friends, saw some incredible landscapes and glaciers, had a famous, gold medal-winning Olympic athlete take part in one of my workshops and had more fun than I had done in years.

The moral of this story is that fear stops us from doing new things. We fear the unknown and we start to imagine what the worst-case scenario will be. You'll only ever really know if you go out there and try something. It might be horrendous but it might just be magnificent. It's like that scary ride at the theme park that you're petrified about going on. Yet straight after the ride is over, you go back to wait in line all over again, because you loved the thrill of it so much.

There's a famous saying by Helen Keller that goes *"life is either a daring adventure or nothing at all"* I'd like to go one better than that: Life is either a daring adventure or a mundane existence with nothing but a lizard for company. I know which one I'd rather choose.

> **"You must give everything to make your life as beautiful as the dreams that dance in your imagination."**

– Roman Payne

Changes I'd like to make...

Notes to self...

Chapter Three

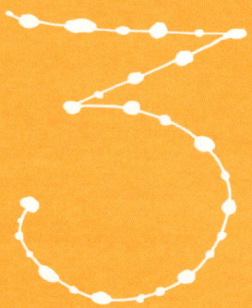

Patience dear one…patience

"Patience is the calm acceptance that things can happen in a different order than the one you have in mind."

– David G. Allen

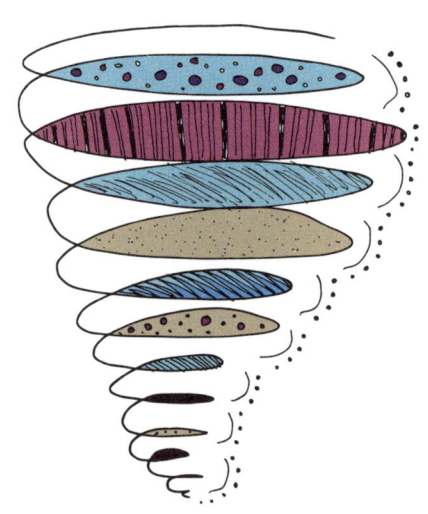

Have you ever wondered why life is never straightforward? The twists and turns we experience along the pathway of our lives are the biggest mysteries of all and sometimes it can be so difficult to wait for the things that we want.

You're in control of your dreams and the actions you can take to make them a reality, but one thing that I am convinced of is this: The Universe is in control of when and how that will happen.

Have you ever tried to force something to move forward in your life and it just won't budge? Maybe you're trying to do that right now and it feels like your feet are stuck in cement. That's because, chances are, you're pushing against the natural order of the Universe, instead of patiently going with the flow.

All in good time, as the saying goes, but it can be very frustrating indeed! Perhaps reading this story will help you endure whatever it is you're waiting for and in the process, let it restore your faith in the gift of patience.

A story about waiting and endurance

Detroit-born soul singer Oliver Cheatham, began singing from an early age. He was very talented and singing was his life.

At the start of his career, he moved from group to group without much success, before finally getting signed to a record label as a solo singer at the age of 35.

His best-performing song 'Get Down Saturday Night' only reached 38th place in the UK and American charts and he lost his recording contract. So, he spent most the 1990s in obscurity, working as a backing singer for other artists.

Oliver's star might have fallen but it would rise again, as luck and destiny were about to play a huge part in his life. 20 years after it was first released, Italian House Music Producer and DJ, Vito Lucente, heard 'Get Down Saturday Night' and decided to remix it using samples of the original, alongside a faster, more modern beat. He tracked Oliver down and they re-wrote the song together, releasing it under the name of Room 5 'Make Luv'. This time the song was a huge hit. It reached number one in the UK music chart and stayed there for four weeks.

In fact, it was to become one of the most played songs of that year, featuring in a Hollywood Movie, a PlayStation game and in the biggest TV advert of the year. Oliver wrote and released a new album with Vito and enjoyed his first taste of big success and stardom at the tender age of 55.

Vito Lucente was just 12 years old when Oliver originally recorded the song. The early format wasn't quite right and the secret sauce that would make it perfect would all happen in divine timing. Oliver could have given up on singing but he believed in himself and kept the faith that this was the right path. He might not have been centre stage, but he continued to do what he loved.

Never give up on your dreams. Even if you have to wait five decades to become an 'overnight' success like Oliver Cheatham. When things don't work out the way you want them to, sometimes life feels cruel, but remember that only the Universe holds all the answers.

What if the dream you are pursuing needs more work? What if the person who can help you achieve your dream hasn't entered your life yet? Consider this: they may not have even been born.

Just trust, have faith in yourself and most of all: allow the stars to align. Have the patience to endure the waiting and re-engineering that often comes with making a big dream unfold.

> "I believe that God gives you hopes and dreams in a size that's too large, so you have something to grow into."

– Lynn A. Robinson

Find the magic in the mundane

> *"I choose to believe that there may be a thousand big moments embedded in this day, waiting to be discovered like tiny shards of gold."*

– Shauna Niequist

Mindfulness has become a major industry, addressing the need to switch our busy brains off from all the noise and constant demands on our senses.

The good news is you don't need to download an app, go on a workshop or buy a book to learn how to be mindful. You just need to stop what you're doing for a moment and take notice of what's really going on around you.

We spend a lot of our time raking over the past and projecting ourselves forward into the future. We often allow our past to haunt us, or wish we could go back and relive it.

We spend so much of our lives looking ahead. What will I have to eat later? Where shall I go this weekend? Whose birthday is coming up? What will I buy them? What's on TV this evening?

Now; this very moment is all we have. Acknowledge it; enjoy it and really live it, because in a flash it will be gone. Designated to a memory; a moment you can never have again.

I love the book 'Eat, Pray, Love' by Elizabeth Gilbert. In one of her anecdotes in the book she talks about mindfulness and being present, using the example of going to a tropical paradise on holiday with a friend. Her friend loved the place they were staying so much, she spent the entire time planning and talking about how great it would be to come back to that location, rather than simply enjoying being there the first time.

How often has this happened to you? Maybe you do this more than you realise. Switching off from fretting about what's going to happen in the next hour, day, week, year, lifetime, allows you to get acquainted with the gift that is going on in the very moment that you're reading this.

I always remember my uncle Jorge, telling me to be mindful long before it was a fashionable thing to do. He lives in Mexico, so I don't get to see him very often. Many years ago, he was the pilot for a large Mexican crystal company and it was his job to fly the executives around the world in the company's private jet. He was a very busy man and never in control of his own schedule. He spent so much time travelling, it was difficult arranging any time to see him. One day, he just happened to be having an unexpected 24-hour stopover in London, so me and my mother jumped on a train and dashed down to London to meet him.

There stood Jorge, larger than life enveloping us in hugs, smiles and his wise cracking sense of humour. *"I'm going to treat you ladies. Where is the best restaurant in London?"* he asked us. I'd always wanted to go to Michael's Cain's restaurant, Langan's Brasserie, so when I tentatively suggested that he immediately whisked us off there. We had the most wonderful afternoon, laughing, catching up with all his news, eating and drinking wine in those glamorous surroundings. I felt very special indeed.

At one point in the proceedings, as I was a little bit tipsy from the wine and on an emotional high from laughing at all his jokes and funny stories, my uncle leaned across to me and whispered *"Just be in this moment Natalia. You'll never have this again. Enjoy it and be aware of how great it is right now; whilst it's happening. Never forget to do that whenever times are good. Enjoy the moment and you'll have it forever."*

I've never forgotten those words or that very sweet moment. Ah, how fabulous are those days when everything feels exciting and special? However, most days aren't like that at all, when you have to endure the grind of daily routine. The insignificant, run-of-the-mill days where nothing in particular stands out in your memory. So how do you find magic in a moment that feels no different to any other?

You have to stop and take notice of 'what is' that's how.

When anything is in plentiful supply it loses its appeal very quickly. Being with my uncle for those few precious hours was magical, but how about if he came to live in the same town as me and I could see him as often as I wished? Would I feel as excited about that once I'd gotten used to him being around all the time? I strongly suspect not. We'd run out of new things to tell one another, mine or his little quirks would probably start getting on one another's nerves. Worse still, if he lived so close by, I'd probably not make it as much of a priority to meet up with him, because I could see him any time I wanted. Therein lies the problem. We take for granted those things that we have an abundance of and crave the things that we see as scarce.

For me, mindfulness is not some mystical formula that you need to study intently, or have passed on to you by a guru. You can be mindful any time you want.

The secret is to see everything for what it really is: precious, special and magical.

One of my guilty pleasures is the TV show 'I'm a Celebrity Get Me Out of Here'. What I find most fascinating about it is, how the people taking part respond when the luxuries of everyday life are stripped away. They go into fits of rapture when they are given a tiny piece of chocolate for the first time in two weeks. Finally, being able to sit in a comfy chair, rather than a tree branch or the jungle floor becomes like a small slice of heaven to them. The simple things that we don't even notice day to day become something major when we no longer have them.

Just a few weeks before I wrote this book, southern Europe experienced some adverse weather conditions and this killed off a large crop of lettuces. The humble lettuce became a thing of scarcity and as soon as word got out, there was immediate panic buying. Many British supermarkets had to limit the number of lettuces sold to each customer, which I found very amusing. Who knew that salad leaves could become something so highly prized?

Right now, I'd like you to stop and focus on something that is around you. As I sit here, I have my ever-present cup of coffee on the table next to me. What is near to you that you're eating, drinking or using in this moment? Imagine if this was the very last time you would ever have this drink, type of food or item? Really take the time to look at it and savour it. Remember: you're never, ever going to be able to have access to it again. What do you notice about its appearance, the design, the colour? If it's an object, are there any little marks or peculiarities about it that make it yours and show its history? If it's food or a drink, notice the unique taste and smell. Take it all in and really pay attention to how this makes you feel.

Doing this and making it a daily ritual - as many times a day as you can – helps you to cut yourself off from dwelling on the past or projecting yourself forward in time, wishing, wanting and waiting. Those few precious moments spent noticing what you have right now and truly appreciating its value, gives you instant access to a greater depth of feeling.

We tend to focus on what we think is important. We constantly hope for magic and search for buried treasure. In reality, if we only took a few moments a day to look around us, we'd see that what we've been wishing about and searching for, was there all along.

If you wait for the good days you'll be waiting forever. No need to wait. The good days are already here. Experience them, cherish them and live them to the full.

"Focus on the present, the daily, the tangible...not on the news headlines but on the flowers growing in your own garden, the children growing in your own home, this way of living has the potential...to yield a glittering handful of diamonds where a second ago there was coal."

– Shauna Niequist

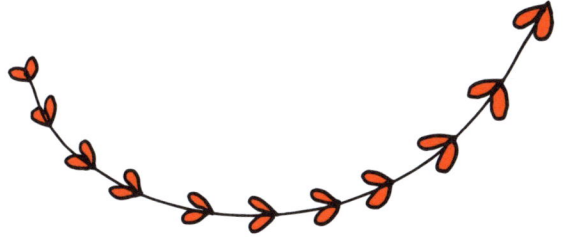

Ways I can be more mindful...

Notes to self...

Chapter Four

Love, love, love

"Your task is not to seek for love,
but merely to seek and find
all the barriers within yourself
that you have built against it."

– Rumi

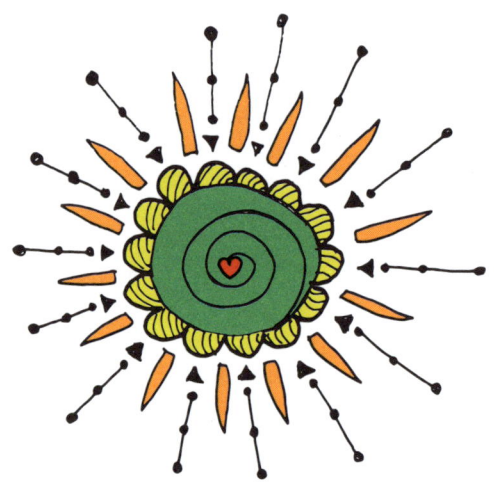

One of the greatest, most fundamental needs of human beings is to be loved. Being deprived of that as a child can be psychologically damaging. Our desire to be loved is incredibly strong and research shows, that feeling loved is one of the biggest boosts to our happiness levels.

Through my work, I've spoken to so many people who aren't in a romantic relationship and would dearly love to be. They say that it's not just about being loved, they want to give their love to someone, to nurture and be as close as possible to another person. Science shows us that whilst being loved fills us with happiness, expressing love to others also gives us the same, great sense of fulfilment.

To love and be loved; both are important but all too often we make it our priority to look for love outside of ourselves. I know this to be true. I spent the first 44 years of my life looking for love and approval from other people. What the Universe did in return was to present me with a mirror; one that reflected my lack of self-love and approval right back at me through my relationships.

These things we go through; broken friendships; toxic relationships; loneliness; they're all part of a series of tests. A test of our commitment to loving ourselves.

The relationship you have with yourself is the most important one of all. You're the person that you'll wake up with every morning and the person whom you'll spend every minute of every day with. It's going to be a long old life if you don't love yourself.

They say you allow others to treat you a little less badly than you treat yourself. So why is that? If you were brought up being told by your parents, siblings, friends, teachers that you are lazy, stupid, overweight, not good enough, a nuisance, unattractive… (insert whatever words you were on the receiving end of) then that's what you believe yourself to be. As you go through life, if you have these limiting beliefs, it's hard to love and approve of yourself. It's especially difficult when things aren't going well or someone reminds you about that limiting belief.

Imagine if you were sitting on a train and a stranger came and sat next to you. Imagine they started to engage you in conversation and pretty soon they began to criticise your clothes, your hair and told you that you looked a complete mess. How would you feel? Even though this person is a complete stranger and you will never see them again, chances are their words would have some effect on you. If you were feeling good about yourself, you might wonder to yourself *"Why on earth did they just say those things? What is that person's problem?"* if your self-esteem was good, then you'd probably go about the rest of your day without giving it much more thought. However, if you'd grown up being told that your dress sense was terrible, the words of this stranger might penetrate and bruise you far more deeply. After all, they're just reinforcing what you believe about yourself, right?

If your dress sense isn't the thing that pushes your pain buttons, then what is? For me it would definitely be my weight. It goes up and down like a yo-yo and I have three different dress sizes of clothes in my wardrobe that I gravitate between. It's not such a big deal, when you look at it in the grand scheme of things, but my family and my school mates teased and harassed me quite a lot about my weight when I was growing up. It's my 'thing' and it knocked my self-confidence and self-love for so many years.

Recently, I found some old photographs from 15 years ago. It was a time when I was much younger and slimmer and I couldn't believe the difference between now and then. I looked amazing. One of the things that struck me was, even though I looked much better then, I still wasn't happy with myself at that time. Now my skin is more wrinkled and my belly is rounder, but I'm so much more content. **I love the wiser, older me.** I feel like Yoda the Jedi Master from the Star Wars movies. Everyone loves him because he knows a thing or two about life. They don't care whether he's the height of fashion or how well preserved his looks are. It's what's on the inside that counts. In fact, one of Yoda's famous sayings is this:

"When nine hundred years old you reach, look as good, you will not, hmmmm? Size matters not. Look at me. Judge me by my size, do you? Hmm? Hmm. And well you should not. For my ally is the force, and a powerful ally it is."

These are superficial things. Weight can be lost, appearances improved upon, but what about the inner things that you feel make you less than loveable. The things that aren't such quick fixes? Perhaps you've made mistakes and the people around you disapproved of this. Maybe you didn't work hard enough, or achieve the things your parents wanted you to and it's made you feel like a failure.

Whatever your 'thing' is, that thing makes you feel less than okay; oh-so-unlovable. It's a heavy old burden to carry around with you. Make a commitment to yourself right here and now, that you'll place it down and remind yourself to stop picking it up and carrying it around with you any longer. **Instead of looking for someone else to fall in love with, how about working on falling in love with yourself.**

If you realised every day, just what a better place you've made the world; if you knew how many different and wonderful ways you've improved people's lives around you; if you could even come close to imagining how much more you have to give, then you wouldn't focus on what other people think is wrong with you. Maybe, just maybe, you'd get up every morning and stand in your magnificence.

You are loveable. Now, go and shine that light of yours as brightly as you possibly can.

> "There is only one true love affair; the one with yourself. All others are expressions of it."

– Hemal Radia

Forgiveness

A few years ago, a very dear friend took me to hear the Dalai Lama in conversation at The Royal Albert Hall. One thing he spoke about during this event has lodged itself firmly in my mind ever since. The gentleman who was hosting the interview asked the Dalai Lama how long he prayed for each day and what his prayers were about. The Dalai Lama said *"I pray for about five hours every morning and I pray a lot for China."* The interviewer was quite shocked and asked *"Why would you pray for China when they have taken over your country and tried to inhibit its culture?"* A big smile spread over the Dalai Lama's face and he replied *"I pray for China because they need compassion the most."*

What if we all took a leaf out of the Dalai Lama's book? **Can you imagine how different things would be if we all chose to see our enemies with compassion instead of resentment?**

Think about someone you don't like very much or whom you feel has wronged you in some way. No matter what they did or how badly things turned out, holding onto resentment towards them and the pain that happened between you, will only make you suffer more.

"The elimination diet: Remove anger, regret, resentment, guilt, blame, and worry. Then watch your health, and life, improve."

– Charles F. Glassman

An exercise in forgiveness

Close your eyes, then picture the face of the person you dislike or are holding resentment towards. Now, imagine them surrounded in a halo of golden light. Wish them well in your thoughts and imagine this image of them dissolving, until you can no longer see this person in your mind's eye.

You may find this difficult to do. That's okay, it's not an instant quick fix. You will probably need to repeat this exercise many times over, until you begin to feel those resentful thoughts towards this person diminishing. It takes a lot of inner work to let go and forgive, but the rewards offer you endless possibilities for more love and light to enter your mind and your heart.

A final word about relationships

> "Everyone wants to ride with you in the limo, but what you want is someone who will take the bus with you when the limo breaks down."

– Oprah Winfrey

When you love and approve of yourself, that's when you're able to look at certain relationships and to ask yourself whether those people deserve to be a part of your life. Everything has a shelf life, even relationships. I'm not just talking about romantic relationships. Business partnerships, friends and acquaintances, even family members all fall into this category. People come into your life for a reason. Enjoy those moments you have with the people close to you and learn all you can during that time, because we're all teachers for one another.

You and everyone around you are constantly changing and growing. Sometimes your purpose for being around someone shifts and the spell is broken. That's when the time comes to release them from your life. You'll know in your heart when that moment has arrived. Sometimes they come back into your life when the time is right and the relationship can begin a new cycle. Other times the closeness you once shared cannot ever be recreated and the relationship is over. Learn to let it go with good grace and just know that interesting and exciting new relationships are waiting to be discovered. This is all part of your evolution. What's meant for you will never pass you by.

> "Sometimes the door closes on a relationship, not because we failed but because something bigger than us says this no longer fits our life. So, lock the door, shed a tear, turn around and look for the new door that's opened. It's a sign that you're no longer that person you were, it's time to change into who you are. It's going to be okay."

– Lee Goff

Notes to self...

Chapter Five

Be authentic

> "I'm like a little boy
> from Virginia.
> I'm a backpacker. In my head,
> I'm left of centre.
> I come from the pool of weirdos."

– Pharrell Williams

Be yourself.

Just be you.

Such an easy thing to say,

Not an easy thing to do.

Your authentic self: it's who you're being when no one else is looking. It's your real face behind the mask you wear.

How comfortable are you about being your true, authentic self?

How much do you care about pleasing others and getting their approval?

What hopes and dreams have you been keeping a lid on and for how long?

The challenge to being your authentic self begins at an early age. Our parents want to protect us. To teach us discipline and right from wrong. These are positive intentions, yet at the same time, in the process of trying to keep us safe, this can put a straitjacket on our authenticity.

We generally want to please our parents or rebel against them. Either way, we can lose sight of what we really want and who we really are on the inside. We make friends, form relationships and work with people who all get acquainted, not with our authentic self, but with the person wearing the mask. That's when it all starts to get out of hand.

Being true to yourself can be painful because the truth hurts. Just who does the truth hurt? Well, it's painful for someone else if they don't want to hear it. It can be scary for someone who knows the mask-wearing version of you, to see what's underneath. It can be equally, if not more painful for you if you feel like you want to please others and not hurt their feelings.

In the beginning, hiding the real you from plain sight gives you an easier life. You don't have to battle and you get to make someone else happy. Never underestimate how seductive that is. Making other people happy feels good. That's until you get further down the road of life and the true you is bursting to free itself. That's when things can get rather painful.

> **"The most important kind of freedom is to be what you really are. There can't be any large-scale revolution until there's a personal revolution, on an individual level. It's got to happen inside first."**

– Jim Morrison

Waiting for the right time to speak up; to unleash the real you onto the world doesn't get easier as time goes on. The longer you wait, the more urgency it gathers and tends to explode out of you rather than calmly rising to the surface. When that happens, everyone around you gets a huge shock and goes *"Woah! What's the matter with you?"* On the inside, you've been like a volcano, whose tectonic plates have been shifting around and the pressure has been building up to this crescendo for years. Then wham! Molten lava pours out everywhere and someone gets burnt.

Have those authentic conversations today, with the ones who matter most, about the things that matter most to you. If you can't or won't have those conversations right now, then think about how and when you'll do it. Whatever you do; make it happen sooner rather than later.

When your authentic self is ready to emerge, just make sure that you're well prepared with a first-aid kit, so you can administer after care for those around you and most importantly for yourself.

Your authentic conversation might be something as simple as: *"Honey, I've always wanted to have a motorbike, so I'm going to get my biker's licence."* Or as big as, *"I've decided I can't do this job any more, it's so stressful and I hate it. I want to retrain and do something I'm passionate about."*

Whatever your truth is, speak up. If it's important to you, then it's important. You don't have to make excuses for being you. Bear in mind that whilst you've been spending time, getting acquainted with the real you under the surface, this authentic you may be a stranger to other people. Be prepared for the aftershock, get ready to listen, have the bandages ready and try to minimise the injury to yourself and the meeter and greeter of your true self.

> **"My voice is never much louder than a ripple, but even small voices sound loud when you talk about things that matter."**

– Natalie Lloyd

Being authentic extends to lots of different aspects of your communication with others. I remember going to an event a few years ago. It was organised by a gentleman whom I'd had a few face-to-face coaching sessions with. I'd also attended some of his meditation events, so we'd met quite a few times in the recent past. He was a very busy man, he worked all over the world and was the author of a best-selling book, so he was used to meeting a lot of people on his travels. As I arrived at this event, there he was greeting everyone as they walked in. He gave me a big hug and as he did so I said *"Hello again! How are you?"* he stepped back, looked at me with a smile and said *"I'm sorry, have we met? I don't remember."* I laughed it off and said *"Yes we have many times, it's okay you could have just pretended you remembered me."* He looked at me with a puzzled expression and said *"Why would I do that? It's always best to be honest."*

This short, seemingly insignificant exchange between me and him hit me like a bolt of lightning. I was projecting onto him the very thing that I had been doing all my life: being inauthentic to please other people. His honesty, his directness was so refreshing that it made me realise what was happening and how, even small white lies add another layer to your mask of inauthenticity. **When you're wearing a mask other people don't know who you are and neither do you.**

So, having said all of this, you may be wondering: is it worth being open, honest and authentic? The answer to this question is always YES, YES, YES!

As Shrek would say *"Better out than in."* It's always better to be open about who you and what you want. Doing this gives you freedom. Keeping a lid on who you are is like having some dark shadow of your own making that stalks you wherever you go. **Get away from the shadows and walk across to the sunny side of the street. It might hurt your eyes at first but it's much warmer and prettier there.**

Come and join me.

Notes to self...

Chapter Six

You are very wise indeed

"At times you have to leave the city of your comfort and go into the wilderness of your intuition. What you'll discover will be wonderful. What you'll discover is yourself."

– Alan Alda

Your intuition is always speaking to you...how carefully are you listening?

You see, your intuition is very gentle. It whispers. It guides and it coaxes. It won't overpower you or force you down a certain path, but it will always tell you what to do for your highest good.

The ego, on the other hand, is like a false identity. It's so complex, that it's hard to define in just a few sentences. Here's my understanding of what the ego is all about.

The ego hides behind the words *"I"* and *"me"* and gets us to believe that our own hype and our worst flaws are what is real. For example: when we talk about being good at things, *"I'm a great tennis player"* or *"I'm a very generous person"*. Equally, when we define ourselves according to whatever we believe is wrong with us or lacking. Such as *"I'm not good at maths"* or *"my curly hair is unattractive."*

It's difficult to describe and define the ego because it's made up of so many different layers. We gather these year upon year and we start to believe that we 'are' our experiences. That we are who other people tell us we are and we allow our emotions to define us too. None of this is real.

When you're connecting with your ego, you feel a strong sense of wanting to be right, to know better or to be better than someone else.

When you connect with your intuition, you're connecting with your highest self. **Your intuition wants what's right for you and what's right for the highest good of all.** It's your authentic self speaking. It's the part of you that considers the whole picture. Your intuition is the best bullshit detector there is. It sees beyond illusion and measures consequences. It grasps the longer-term implications not just the present moment. It uncovers the pretty façade, and asks you to take the path that is best for you, not the easiest one; not the one that looks good to others or the route that gives you short-term gain.

Your intuition digs much deeper to get to the core of a situation and urges you to act with integrity.

You may be thinking *"how can I tell the difference between my ego speaking to me and my intuition guiding me?"* There is a world of difference between the intentions of your ego and your intuition. The more accustomed you've become to listening to your ego, the trickier it will be to sense what your intuition is telling you.

Your intuition speaks to you through your gut.
When someone or something is 'off', you'll know it by that funny feeling in your stomach. Some people describe it as a fluttering feeling. For me my stomach feels tight, as though the empty space has suddenly been filled by some entity, gently summoning my attention. Learn to take notice of how it feels for you.

The ego approaches things more aggressively.
That's why the ego is a lot more noticeable and tends to grab your attention to get what it wants. It shouts and screams at you. It tries to make you rationalise; to make complexity appear simple.

Your intuition is much more subtle.
It beckons you; it dances a thought across your mind. It creates a flicker of something that seems important and disappears as quickly as it came. Intuition often has no rationale other than a thought or a feeling, that just 'feels right'.

When you learn to notice the difference, and trust your gut instinct – even if you can't explain it – that's when you can begin to work in harmony with it.

Your intuition is speaking to you when…

You feel uncomfortable. After a while, if its gentle messages don't provoke you into action, what else can your intuition do but start cranking up the pain? If your life feels out of balance, if you feel stuck, lethargic, unwell, uncomfortable in your own skin, then maybe you need to start paying attention to this and ask yourself *"What am I not doing?"* Your intuition will quite gladly give you the answers, when you're ready to begin hearing them.

You feel like you're wearing a mask, or as though you don't fit in. When the people you're surrounded by start making you feel like there's something wrong with you, that's when your intuition is politely telling you *"it's time to leave the party."*

When you nurture the connection with your intuition; when you trust it like the dearest friend and the wisest sage you'll ever know, it will always be your most faithful servant.

If you want to change your life, start creating the stillness that allows your intuition to surface. This can only happen when you silence your mind chatter. There is an ancient saying by the Zen masters: *"You cannot see your reflection in running water, only in water that is still."*

Think about where and how you can create stillness in your life every day, even if it's only for a few moments. My daughter was born in the year 2000 and her generation have grown up surrounded by technology, the number one gadget being the smart phone which offers 24-hour entertainment. If I glance at her when she's watching a DVD, chances are she'll have her laptop open so she can surf the internet and her mobile phone will be constantly chiming with messages, as she simultaneously chats with several friends. She's like many modern teenagers, doing so many things at once and not concentrating on any one of them in particular.

You might not be a teenager anymore, but think for a moment about how your life is crowded by gadgets, noise and entertainment. Consider how often you do two things at once, such as eating whilst reading a book or magazine, exercising whilst listening to music or watching TV and catching up on social media.

Try, even for just for a few minutes each day, to do one thing in isolation. When you're having lunch, concentrate on the food you're eating. Savour every mouthful, enjoy the flavours and chew more slowly. If you're watching TV, switch your phone off, or leave it in another room until the programme has finished. That way you can fully concentrate and enjoy whatever it is you're watching. This is being mindful and mindfulness equals peacefulness.

One of the most effective ways to silence the chatter of your ego and allow your intuition to speak to you is through meditation. It's a beautiful way to go inward. You don't need to force yourself to sit cross-legged on a rock for hours to feel the benefits. If you can set aside just 5 or 10 minutes each day to be still, to concentrate on your breathing and to relax your body, you will notice just how much calmer and more contented this makes you feel. A lot of people say they cannot meditate and that is like saying *"I can't run a marathon"* or *"I don't know how to play chess"*. No one is born being able to do those things automatically, they take practice and dedication. The same is true of meditation. Your mind and body are so used to being active. To sit still and do nothing will probably feel extremely alien to you at first. I can assure you of this: the more you meditate the more you'll begin to enjoy it and feel the benefits.

I'll leave you with one of my favourite quotes about meditation and mindfulness:

> **"If the ocean can calm itself, so can you. We are both salt water mixed with air."**

– Nayyirah Waheed

"When Intuition moved in, she washed all the windows, cleaned out the fireplace, planted fruit trees, and lit purple candles. She doesn't have many possessions. Each thing is special. Since Intuition moved in, my life has been turned inside out."

– J Ruth Gelder – The Book of Qualities

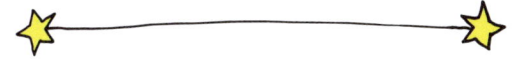

Ways I can create stillness...

Notes to self...

Chapter Seven

Keeping the light on

"You know what's just as powerful as a good cup of coffee in the morning? Starting your day with some good, loving thoughts. It can change how your whole day unfolds."

– Karen Salmansohn

I get in my own way. Do you do that too?

I tell myself I'm not good enough and although I do it less and less these days, it still happens.

When I decided to write 'The Little Book of Love and Light', I had a moment where the conversation between myself and my ego went something like this:

"Who's going to want to read your book?"
"Who do you think you are?"
"What makes you think people will buy it"
"What makes you think people will enjoy it?"

Thankfully, I've been around my ego long enough to know its foibles. It can be a great big bully. It tries to scare me and it's succeeded so many times, but not anymore. I've learned all of its moves and I'm ready for it. I know exactly what to do and say. When my ego roars at me, I roar right back:

"I'm doing this and I'm going to find out for myself thank you very much. Now, get out of my way."

That's what you've got to do too because your ego doesn't like it much when you push back. It shrinks and retreats into the shadows where it came from. It's a vampire. A creature of the darkness, that hates having the light shone on it. The best thing to do is to keep the light on at all times.

Sometimes your world will be naturally light and bright, with sunshine pouring in through every window. Then there are those days; you know the ones I'm talking about. The days when the darkness sneaks in. When so much feels wrong. Those moments when you feel the lifeforce being sucked right out of you. That's when you must reach for the light switch.

All the chapters in this book represent turning on a different light, so go back and read the ones that feel like they will have most meaning and impact right now.

This chapter is a quick way to revisit the different themes throughout the book and to illuminate whatever light might be fading within you. Here are four activities that provide an instant way to lift your mood and give you a positive energy boost.

1. Positive affirmations

Let's begin with some positive affirmations. These are short sentences with long-lasting impact that will act as a constant source of light when you repeat them often enough. They serve to create your reality and to remind you to feel gratitude.

The affirmations I'm sharing here are ones that I use all the time. They are inspired by the affirmations of some of my favourite gurus like Louise L. Hay, Esther and Jerry Hicks and Doreen Virtue. Repetition is the key to success. Identify the ones you like best and that have most meaning and write them on little cards of Post-It notes. Why not create your own? Always write them in the present tense, because you already have or are on the way to possessing everything you wish for.

                 I am talented. Nothing can stop me.

                 My dreams are achievable.

                 I am my own best friend.

My only job in life is to be who I really am.

♡

My skills and talents are needed in the world.

♡

I am a money magnet.

♡

My intuition is loud and clear. I trust myself.

♡

I am exactly where I need to be.

♡

Success follows me wherever I go.

♡

Challenges are opportunities for me to grow.

♡

I am divinely guided and protected.

♡

There is no shortage of time.

My life is an exciting adventure.

♡

I never give up on what I know in my heart
is right for me.

♡

I am loveable. Love flows back to me
one hundred times over.

♡

I am unique and special.
There is no one else like me.

♡

I am worthy of every blessing that is coming my way.

♡

Magic happens when I embrace every possibility.

♡

I am brave. Nothing can stop me.

♡

I am enough.

"When you are joyful, when you say yes to life and have fun and project positivity all around you, you become a sun in the centre of every constellation, and people want to be near you."

– Shannon L. Alder

2. Gratitude journaling

Research shows that when we express gratitude every day, we sleep better, we enjoy better health and we feel happier. A few years ago I took part in something called the 'Happiness Project'. I received an email every day for 30 days reminding me to think of three things I was grateful for that day. Doing this made me much more aware of the seemingly small things that went on around me and made me realise how important it is to appreciate them.

The most significant thing about taking part in this project was making it a habit. That repetition worked for me and it has become a ritual I perform every day. It's not always easy to be grateful. Some days when life is throwing me curved balls I have to dig very deep. That's where the real blessing comes from daily gratitude. This yields, as author Shauna Neiquist so elegantly puts it, *"a glittering handful of diamonds where a second ago there was coal."* That's when you're truly appreciating your life and living it to its fullest.

Here are two ways to express gratitude. You may wish to copy these pages or use a notebook or journal to record the things you're grateful for. Writing this down is a wonderful way of keeping a record you can look back on. A perfect reminder of all the abundance you have in your life.

Today, I am grateful for...

Today's date: /   /

1.

2.

3.

Today, I am excited about...

Today's date: /   /

1.

2.

3.

Keeping the light on

3. Rewarding yourself

A big part of becoming your own best friend is learning to treat yourself like the precious soul that you are. Imagine yourself as the most amazing friend you've ever had. Someone who is unique and special; a person who has been through so much and is a complete inspiration to you. The warmest, kindest and most loving person you will ever meet.

You are all of these things…do you realise how amazing that makes you? As your own best friend, it's important to show that gratitude towards yourself in the ways that you enjoy most. To honour yourself.

Think about the things you enjoy receiving as gifts or gestures from other people. That might be a bunch of flowers, enjoying afternoon tea, a new music CD by your favourite artist, or slipping into a hot bubbly bath surrounded by scented candles.

Don't wait to be rewarded by others. Treat yourself to the things you love most. You won't disappoint yourself because you know that whatever gift you give yourself will be something you'll really like.

Now take some time to think about the things you'd love to receive and list 20 different ideas. The ideas might not come to you all at once. Do give this some thought and revisit and update your list.

Remember: you don't have to spend a lot of money to make yourself feel special. Take a look at this list whenever you need a boost. Select something from it and go ahead and pamper yourself with whatever you've chosen. Then sit back and enjoy how good this makes you feel.

20 Treats just for me...

1.
2.
3.
4.
5.
6.
7.
8.
9.
10.
11.
12.
13.
14.
15.
16.
17.
18.
19.
20.

4. Overcoming self-doubt

Throughout this book, the topic of self-doubt has arisen a few times. No matter how positive or successful a person is, everyone suffers from self-doubt at one time or another. The most important thing about self-doubt is to acknowledge it will come up to the surface sooner or later and to have a mechanism to cope with it. One that quashes it and stops it from damaging your self-esteem or getting in the way of your progress.

Doubt comes up when we look to the future through the lens of the past. One of the best ways I've found of helping me to overcome self-doubt and fear is to ask myself some questions.

For example, I spent years avoiding launching my own jewellery line because I told myself it was too competitive and too expensive to do. It was only when I challenged my doubts and pushed back at them that I discovered the truth. I asked myself: *"Just how competitive is the jewellery design marketplace?"* *"How expensive will it be to create my own jewellery?"*

I realised that I didn't have the answers to those questions. I was making assumptions. I went away and did some thorough research. I challenged my assumptions and I found that yes, one of them was true. The market is extremely competitive, but there was also a huge demand for hand-designed jewellery. There was an audience for my work as long as I knew who they were and what they wanted. One of my most enlightening discoveries was this: I found that having my jewellery pieces cast in precious metals was nowhere near as expensive as I thought. This created great possibility, where before there was only doubt and fear.

When you make up the rest of the story without getting the real answers then you're deceiving yourself. Imagine if you did this every time doubt cropped up? Do you want to live a life based on half-truths?

If you want to get out of your own way and meet self-doubt head on, here is a checklist you can follow. Use this each time self-doubt creeps in, to challenge your assumptions and uncover the truth.

I hope you find this helpful and remember: if you're finding your doubts too invasive to stand back from, then speak to someone else about them and get an outsider's opinion. We're sometimes too close and too embroiled in our own issues that we need a fresh pair of eyes to help us see what's real and what isn't. Oh and do you recall that virtual tribe we talked about in Chapter 1? Don't forget to ask for your guru's opinion too.

Self-doubt checklist...

What am I telling myself about this situation?

What is the truth?

What do I need to find out?

What would my virtual tribe members say about this?

"I think that we are like stars. Something happens to burst us open; but when we burst open and think we are dying; we're actually turning into a supernova. And then when we look at ourselves again, we see that we're suddenly more beautiful than we ever were before!"

– C. JoyBell C.

Acknowledgements, Hugs and Kisses...

It takes a village to create a book and I'm so blessed to have one heck of a village behind me. In the spirit of gratitude, I have so many people to thank.

To my precious Mr Loveday. You put up with my nit-pickiness and seemed to somehow enjoy pulling rabbits out of hats when it came to the design of this book. From cover to cover, you spent endless time making sure every part of it was just right. Your patience, your skill and your faith in me kept this project going even on the darkest of days. Thank you from the bottom of my heart.

Thank you to my Mum and Norman, and my crowd of Kickstarter backers who helped bring this book into the world. Your belief in my idea and your generosity blows me away. I cannot thank you enough for your pledges, your support and your encouragement.

To my daughter, Estella. You are my inspiration when it comes to love and light. Anyone who is lucky enough to meet you gets to see your loveliness and just how brightly you shine. Thank you also for being a very patient and diligent proof reader.

A big thanks to my dear friend, Liz Welch. You've shown me what being mindful is all about. Your creativity and the way you live your life is an inspiration to everyone.

To Eddie Loveday who filmed and edited the video that launched this book out into the world. Thank you so much for your support. I can't wait to see how your story unfolds. You have a very bright future ahead of you.

I need to say an extra-big thank you to all of my 'Angel Club' ladies. You're the first ones to know about all my kooky ideas and you're my chief sounding board. I love the way we've connected and how we support one another every day through our Facebook Group. I'm honoured to call you my friends.

Finally, I must thank my tribe. They are amazing and you, dear reader, are part of that tribe. You are one of the like-minded souls I've been searching for all my life and I'm thrilled to have found you. Let's celebrate our uniqueness and always reach out to one another, even if we can only do this in our thoughts and through the pages of this book. I know you, I love you and I have your back. Every time you're doubting yourself, imagine me rooting for you to get out of your own way and to fulfil your potential. You've got this. You've always had it. I believe in you.

Resources & Further Information

Books that I love and you might just enjoy too.

The Alchemist
Paolo Coelho

Loveability
Robert Holden

The Miracle of Mindfulness
Thich Nhat Hanh

Peace and Plenty
Sarah Ban Breathnach

What I Know for Sure
Oprah Winfrey

The Wise Heart
Jack Kornfield

Simple Abundance: A Daybook of Comfort and Joy
Sarah Ban Breathnach

You Can Heal Your Life
Louise L. Hay

About the Designer

Keith Loveday is a branding expert and graphic designer. He cut his teeth in the design world long before the Apple Mac was king, so he knows a thing or two about typography and the principles of engaging design.
Contact Keith at: **keith@keithloveday.co.uk**
www.keithloveday.co.uk

About the Author

Natalia would love to hear from you!

The Little Book of Love & Light is also available as an online workshop. Natalia presents a range of talks and face-to-face workshops called **'A Day of Love & Light'**.

To find out more about her work and upcoming projects visit her website **www.by-natalia.com** or email her at: **info@stylespecialists.co.uk**